EXPLORING COUNTRIES

Argentina

BLAINE WISEMAN

MEDIA ENHANCED BOOKS

AV2 BY WEIGL™

ADDED VALUE • AUDIO VISUAL

www.av2books.com

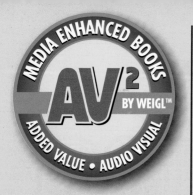

AV² provides enriched content that supplements and complements this book. Weigl's AV² books strive to create inspired learning and engage young minds in a total learning experience.

Your AV² Media Enhanced books come alive with...

Audio
Listen to sections of the book read aloud.

Key Words
Study vocabulary, and complete a matching word activity.

Video
Watch informative video clips.

Quizzes
Test your knowledge.

Embedded Weblinks
Gain additional information for research.

Slide Show
View images and captions, and prepare a presentation.

Go to www.av2books.com, and enter this book's unique code.

BOOK CODE

J354698

Try This!
Complete activities and hands-on experiments.

... and much, much more!

AV² by Weigl brings you media enhanced books that support active learning.

Published by AV² by Weigl
350 5th Avenue, 59th Floor
New York, NY 10118
Websites: www.av2books.com   www.weigl.com

Library of Congress Cataloging-in-Publication Data

Wiseman, Blaine.
 Argentina / Blaine Wiseman.
    pages cm. — (Exploring countries)
Includes index.
ISBN 978-1-4896-3050-6 (hard cover : alk. paper) — ISBN 978-1-4896-3051-3 (soft cover : alk. paper) —
ISBN 978-1-4896-3052-0 (single user ebook) — ISBN 978-1-4896-3053-7 (multi-user ebook)
1. Argentina—Juvenile literature. 2. Argentina—Description and travel—Juvenile literature. I. Title.
F2808.2.W57 2014
982—dc23

                              2014038994

Printed in the United States of America in Brainerd, Minnesota
1 2 3 4 5 6 7 8 9 19 18 17 16 15

012015
WEP160115

Project Coordinator Heather Kissock
Art Director Terry Paulhus

Photo Credits
Every reasonable effort has been made to trace ownership and to obtain permission to reprint copyright material. The publishers would be pleased to have any errors or omissions brought to their attention so that they may be corrected in subsequent printings.

Weigl acknowledges Getty Images as its primary image supplier for this title.

Contents

Argentina Overview

Argentina is located on the southern part of the continent of South America. It is the second-largest country, after Brazil, and the largest Spanish-speaking nation in South America. Argentina has towering mountains, vast plains, rivers, and a long, rugged coastline. The **economy** of Argentina is one of the largest in South America. Many people depend on natural resources for food and jobs. The country's culture was formed by European and American influences. Music, dancing, sports, and politics are all major parts of Argentine life.

In Argentina, llamas are used for their meat and wool. People also use llamas to transport heavy items.

Mount Fitzroy in the Patagonia region is also known as Chaltén. Indigenous people called the peak *Chaltén*, or "smoking mountain," because it looked like a volcano.

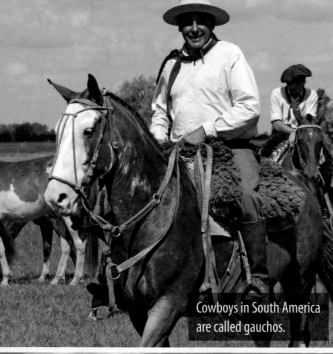

Cowboys in South America are called gauchos.

Buenos Aires has traditional and modern structures. The Puente de la Mujer, or Woman's Bridge, was designed in 2001 by Santiago Calatrava of Spain.

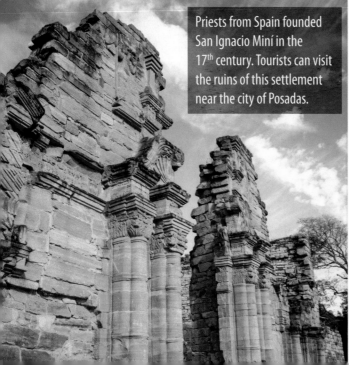

Priests from Spain founded San Ignacio Miní in the 17th century. Tourists can visit the ruins of this settlement near the city of Posadas.

Exploring
Argentina

Covering a total area of 1,073,518 square miles (2,780,400 square kilometers), Argentina is the eighth-largest country in the world. Its shape is an upside-down triangle. The country stretches 2,360 miles (3,800 km) from north to south. At its widest point from east to west, Argentina extends for 880 miles (1,420 km).

Argentina borders the countries of Brazil and Uruguay to the northeast, Bolivia and Paraguay to the north, and Chile to the west. Most of the eastern part of Argentina borders the Atlantic Ocean. The country's coastline, about 2,900 miles (4,700 km) long, is South America's third longest.

Mount Aconcagua

Pacific Ocean

Patagonia

N

Map Legend

 Argentina

 Land

Water

 Rio de la Plata

 Mount Aconcagua

 Patagonia

 Capital City

SCALE

500 Miles

500 Kilometers

Mount Aconcagua

Mount Aconcagua is part of the Andes, the world's longest mountain range. The mountain reaches 22,831 feet (6,959 meters) above sea level. Mount Aconcagua is the highest peak in the **Western Hemisphere**.

Buenos Aires

Bolivia

Brazil

Paraguay

Uruguay

Atlantic Ocean

Chile

Buenos Aires

ENTINA

Patagonia

Falkland Islands

Rio de la Plata

Patagonia

The Argentine part of Patagonia covers 260,000 square miles (675,000 sq. km). Patagonia offers many of Argentina's most beautiful landscapes, from grasslands to **glaciers**. It is also home to many types of plants and animals, including cacti and penguins.

Rio de la Plata

The Rio de la Plata, or "River of Silver," is 180 miles (290 km) long. It is not really a river, but an **estuary** of the Paraná and Uruguay Rivers. This river system drains about one-fifth of South America.

Buenos Aires

Buenos Aires is Argentina's capital and largest city. Sometimes called the "Paris of South America," Buenos Aires is known for its rich culture, history, and **architecture**. Located about 150 miles (240 km) from the Atlantic Ocean, Buenos Aires is on the shore of the Rio de la Plata.

LAND AND CLIMATE

Argentina features a variety of land forms, including rainforests, swamps, grasslands, **plateaus**, and beaches. The large country has four main natural regions. They are the northern region of the Gran Chaco and Mesopotamia, the Pampas, Patagonia, and the Andes.

The Gran Chaco is a basin, or lowland area, that stretches into Paraguay and Bolivia. The Gran Chaco includes forests, grasslands, and wetlands. East of the Gran Chaco, bordered by the Paraná and Uruguay Rivers, is the area called Mesopotamia. In Greek, the word *mesopotamia* means "between two rivers."

Pampas means "flat surface" in the local Quechua Indian language.

Farther south is the Pampas. The western part of the Pampas is known as the dry zone. Deserts and **salt plains** dominate the landscape. In the eastern zone, rainfall is more plentiful.

Iguaçu Falls is made up of hundreds of waterfalls on the Iguaçu River near the border of Argentina and Brazil. The biggest waterfall in Argentina is called the Garganta del Diablo, or Devil's Throat. The falls are protected by national parks in Argentina and Brazil.

Tierra del Fuego is home to Ushuaia, the southernmost city in the world. Millions of tourists come to this city. From here, people set out to trek through the wilderness. Others tour the bays, canals, islands, and channels to see Tierra del Fuego's wildlife. Tourists can even take a cruise to Antarctica from Ushuaia.

High in the Andes, the town of San Carlos de Bariloche sits on the shores of Lake Nahuel Huapi. Hikers and mountain climbers visit in the summer. In the winter, Bariloche becomes Argentina's most popular ski resort.

Glaciares National Park in the Andes is home to more than 240 glaciers. Perito Moreno is one of the largest and is increasing in size. The park's tallest peak, Mount Fitzroy, measures 11,073 feet (3,375 m) high.

Iguaçu Falls vary in height from 200 to 270 feet (60 to 82 m).

INDUSTRY

A rgentina's economy depends on manufacturing, agriculture, and services. More than 100 years ago, farming and ranching, along with metal mining, made Argentina one of the richest countries in the world. Today, 23 percent of its workers are employed in various manufacturing industries. Factories process beef and beef goods, produce clothes and other **textiles**, and manufacture motor vehicles and machinery.

Farming and ranching, forestry, and fishing all contribute to the Argentine economy. Ranchers and farmers raise cattle, sheep, chickens, goats, and pigs. Sheep in the Patagonia grasslands have helped make Argentina one of the world's biggest producers of wool. Beef and leather from Argentine cattle are known around the world for their high quality. Wheat, corn, and soybeans are some of the nation's largest crops.

Today, Argentina is the leading producer of natural gas in South America. The country sends natural gas to its neighbors Chile and Uruguay. It is also South America's fourth-largest petroleum producer.

48 Million
Number of cattle in Argentina.

17 Million
Number of workers in Argentina.

17,900 Miles
Total length of Argentina's natural gas pipelines. (28,800 km)

More than 2 million vehicles in Argentina run on natural gas. That is more than any other country in South America.

POLITICS AND GOVERNMENT

I ndependence in 1816 was followed by years of civil war in Argentina. Finally, the country's first **constitution** was written in 1853. Today, Argentina is officially known as the Argentine **Republic**.

Over the years, even as a republic, Argentina has often been ruled by **dictators**. Juan Perón, a military leader who became popular with many of the country's workers, was elected president in 1946. He was overthrown in a **coup d'état** in 1955. Soon after returning to power almost 20 years later, Perón died, and his third wife, Isabel, followed him in office. Two years later, the military leader Jorge Rafaél Videla took control and ruled the country until 1983. During this time, government officials kidnapped, tortured, and killed as many as 30,000 people who criticized or opposed the government. These victims were later called the "disappeared ones." After Argentina lost a war to Great Britain over the Falkland Islands in 1982, the country returned to **democracy**.

The president, elected every four years, is the head of government. The National Congress, or legislature, includes the Senate, with 72 members, and the Chamber of Deputies, with 257. Argentina is made up of 23 provinces and the city of Buenos Aires. Each province has its own government, which handles local issues.

The legislature meets in the Palace of the National Congress in Buenos Aires. The building was constructed in 1906.

18 and 70
Ages between which an Argentine must vote in national elections.

2007
Year Argentina's first elected female president, Cristina Fernandez, took office.

1946–1952
Years Eva Peron, Juan Perón's second wife, served as First Lady, working to help the poor and increase women's voting rights.

CULTURAL GROUPS

Argentina is made up of many cultural groups. Early settlers from Spain began having children with indigenous people. This created a culture of people with European and indigenous backgrounds. They are called mestizos. In the centuries after Spanish settlement, people from all parts of the world have come to live in Argentina, joining the country's cultural mix.

In the past, many **immigrants** to Argentina came from Italy. Between 1882 and 1920, more than one million Italians came to Argentina looking for work and land. Italians have influenced Argentine culture in many ways, including the language, food, and arts. Today, about 20 million Argentines are descended from Italians.

In Argentina, street signs are written in Spanish, the country's official language.

Some indigenous peoples in Argentina continue to live in their own communities.

The first rugby club in Argentina was formed in 1864, and the sport has been popular ever since. Argentine children begin playing rugby as young as five years old. At the 2007 Rugby World Cup, the national team, the Pumas, finished in third place, which was its highest finish ever.

Ranchers and farmers on the plains of Argentina began playing the sport of polo more than 100 years ago. In polo, horseback riders use long-handled mallets to drive a wooden ball through a goal. The wide-open spaces of the countryside offer the perfect environment for polo. Children begin by learning to ride horses, and they are often playing polo by the age of seven.

Another popular national sport in Argentina is called *pato*, or "duck" in Spanish. Pato players ride horses and try to throw a leather ball, called the duck, through the other team's goal. The game combines elements of polo and basketball.

Juan Martin Zubia of Argentina plays on the national polo team.

3 Number of Argentine tennis players who have won U.S. Open singles championships. Those players were Guillermo Vilas in 1977, Gabriela Sabatini in 1990, and Juan Martin del Potro in 2009.

91 World-record number of goals scored by Lionel Messi in 2012.

2018 Year the Summer Youth Olympics will be held in Buenos Aires.

Mapping Argentina

W e use many tools to interpret maps and to understand the locations of features such as cities, states, lakes, and rivers. The map below has many tools to help interpret information on the map of Argentina.

Map of Argentina

Pacific Ocean

70°W   60°W   50°W

30°S

•Cordoba

Mount Aconcagua

•Mendoza

Buenos Aires ☆

Rio Negro

40°S

Atlantic Ocean

50°S

Falkland Islands

Strait of Magellan

.Ushuaia

MAP LEGEND

★ Capital City
● City
◌ Body of Water

╱ River
-·-·- Country Border
▲ Mountains

╲ Longitude & Latitude
▨ Argentina
▨ Other Countries

N
W   E
S

SCALE

0   500 Miles

0   500 Kilometers

Mapping Tools

- The compass rose shows north, south, east, and west. The points in between represent northeast, northwest, southeast, and southwest.
- The map scale shows that the distances on a map represent much longer distances in real life. If you measure the distance between objects on a map, you can use the map scale to calculate the actual distance in miles or kilometers between those two points.
- The lines of latitude and longitude are long lines that appear on maps. The lines of latitude run east to west and measure how far north or south of the equator a place is located. The lines of longitude run north to south and measure how far east or west of the Prime Meridian a place is located. A location on a map can be found by using the two numbers where latitude and longitude meet. This number is called a coordinate and is written using degrees and direction. For example, the city of Buenos Aires would be found at 35°S and 58°W on a map.

Map It!

Using the map and the appropriate tools, complete the activities below.

Locating with latitude and longitude
1. Which body of water is located at 52°S and 68°W?
2. Which mountain is located at 32°S and 70°W?
3. Which city is found at 54°S and 68°W?

Distances between points
4. Using the map scale and a ruler, calculate the approximate distance between Buenos Aires and Mendoza.
5. Using the map scale and a ruler, calculate the approximate distance between Cordoba and Ushuaia.
6. Using the map scale and a ruler, calculate the approximate length of the Rio Negro.

ANSWERS 1. Strait of Magellan 2. Mount Aconcagua 3. Ushuaia 4. 590 miles (950 km) 5. 1,630 miles (2,625 km) 6. 340 miles (550 km)

Argentina 29

Quiz Time

Test your knowledge of Argentina by answering these questions.

1 On which continent is Argentina located?

2 What city is the capital of Argentina?

3 Which region's name means "between two rivers"?

4 How many species of birds can be found in Argentina?

5 What ski town is on the shores of Lake Nahuel Huapi?

6 What indigenous people lived in Tierra del Fuego?

7 Which empire conquered parts of Argentina before Europeans arrived?

8 What is the longest river in Argentina?

9 What is the second-most-common language spoken in Argentina?

10 Who scored two goals for Argentina in the final game at the 1978 World Cup?

Key Words

architecture: the style in which buildings are designed

censorship: examining publications or films and removing anything that is considered harmful or objectionable

conquistadors: Spanish conquerors

constitution: a written document stating a country's basic principles and laws

coup d'état: a sudden overthrow of a government, bringing a new group into power

democracy: a type of government in which people choose their leaders by voting

dictators: leaders who have complete power over their people and who may govern in a cruel or unfair way

economy: the wealth and resources of a country or area

estuary: a place where the ocean flows up the mouth of a river

European Union: a economic and political organization of 28 countries

fossil fuels: fuels such as coal, natural gas, and oil that formed from the remains of plants and animals that lived long ago

glaciers: large slow-moving sheets of ice

immigrants: people who move to a new country or area to live

imports: goods brought in from another country

life expectancy: the number of years that a person can expect to live

minerals: natural substances that are neither plants nor animals, such as gold, diamond, or iron ore

plateaus: high flat areas of land

republic: a type of government in which the people elect the country's head of state

rodents: animals with large front teeth that they use for gnawing

rural: relating to the countryside

salt plains: flat areas covered with deposits from a body of salt water

species: groups of individuals with common characteristics

textiles: woven or knit cloths

UNESCO: the United Nations Educational, Scientific, and Cultural Organization, whose main goals are to promote world peace and eliminate poverty through education, science, and culture

viceroyalties: districts or provinces governed by a leader called a viceroy

Western Hemisphere: the half of Earth that includes North America, Central America, and South America

Index

Log on to www.av2books.com

AV² by Weigl brings you media enhanced books that support active learning. Go to www.av2books.com, and enter the special code found on page 2 of this book. You will gain access to enriched and enhanced content that supplements and complements this book. Content includes video, audio, weblinks, quizzes, a slide show, and activities.

AV² Online Navigation

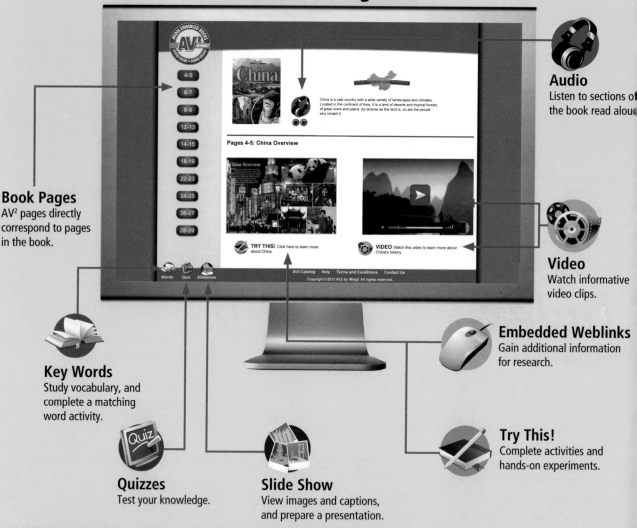

Book Pages
AV² pages directly correspond to pages in the book.

Audio
Listen to sections of the book read aloud

Video
Watch informative video clips.

Key Words
Study vocabulary, and complete a matching word activity.

Embedded Weblinks
Gain additional information for research.

Quizzes
Test your knowledge.

Slide Show
View images and captions, and prepare a presentation.

Try This!
Complete activities and hands-on experiments.

AV² was built to bridge the gap between print and digital. We encourage you to tell us what you like and what you want to see in the future.

Sign up to be an AV² Ambassador at www.av2books.com/ambassador.